A HEALTHY LIFE

Being Social

by Kirsten Chang

BLASTOFF! READERS

BELLWETHER MEDIA • MINNEAPOLIS, MN

Blastoff! Readers are carefully developed by literacy experts to build reading stamina and move students toward fluency by combining standards-based content with developmentally appropriate text.

Level 1 provides the most support through repetition of high-frequency words, light text, predictable sentence patterns, and strong visual support.

Level 2 offers early readers a bit more challenge through varied sentences, increased text load, and text-supportive special features.

Level 3 advances early-fluent readers toward fluency through increased text load, less reliance on photos, advancing concepts, longer sentences, and more complex special features.

★ **Blastoff! Universe**

Reading Level

Beginners

Grade
K

**Grades
1–3**

**Grade
4**

This edition first published in 2022 by Bellwether Media, Inc.

No part of this publication may be reproduced in whole or in part without written permission of the publisher. For information regarding permission, write to Bellwether Media, Inc., Attention: Permissions Department, 6012 Blue Circle Drive, Minnetonka, MN 55343.

Library of Congress Cataloging-in-Publication Data

LC record for Being Social available at https://lccn.loc.gov/2021041260

Text copyright © 2022 by Bellwether Media, Inc. BLASTOFF! READERS and associated logos are trademarks and/or registered trademarks of Bellwether Media, Inc.

Editor: Rebecca Sabelko   Designer: Andrea Schneider

Printed in the United States of America, North Mankato, MN.

Table of Contents

Friendly Faces

Jon meets new friends. They share toys and play. It is fun being social!

Why Is Being Social Important?

Being social is a good way to make friends.

Friends help us stay healthy. They help us feel happier.

Friends give help when we need it. They **support** us.

Being social teaches us **empathy**. We learn to think about others.

How Does Being Social Help?

make friends   feel happier   learn empathy

13

We could become **lonely** without friends.

How Are We Social?

Mia asks if she can play with the group. She makes friends!

Leah shares a snack
with Kai. They smile.
They are being social.

Tools for Being Social

asking to play

smiling

listening ears

19

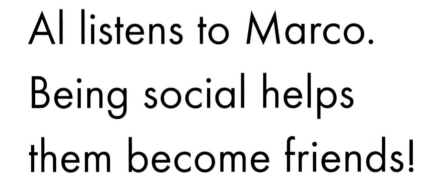

Al listens to Marco. Being social helps them become friends!

Glossary

empathy

the understanding of other people's feelings

support

to help someone by being kind to them during a difficult time

lonely

feeling unhappy because you are alone

To Learn More

AT THE LIBRARY

Chang, Kirsten. *I Am Generous*. Minneapolis, Minn.: Bellwether Media, 2020.

Nelson, Penelope. *Having Empathy*. Minneapolis, Minn.: Jump!, 2020.

Payne, Lauren Murphy. *We Can Get Along: A Child's Book of Choices*. Minneapolis, Minn.: Free Spirit Publishing, 2015.

ON THE WEB

FACTSURFER

Factsurfer.com gives you a safe, fun way to find more information.

1. Go to www.factsurfer.com.

2. Enter "being social" into the search box and click 🔍.

3. Select your book cover to see a list of related content.

Index

The images in this book are reproduced through the courtesy of: Kamira, front cover (happy kids); matthew25, front cover (park); Sergey Novikov, pp. 3, 4-5; MJTH, pp. 6-7; Africa Studio, pp. 8-9; MNStudio, pp. 10-11; Tetra Images, LLC/ Alamy, pp. 12-13; Monkey Business Images, p. 13 (friends); FatCamera, p. 13 (feel happier); Lopolo, p. 13 (learn empathy); wavebreakmedia, pp. 14-15, 22 (lonely); SolStock, pp. 16-17; fizkes, pp. 18-19; Twinsterphoto, p. 19 (asking to play); Juice Flair, p. 19 (smiling); Prostock-studio/ Alamy, p. 19 (listening ears); Yobro10, pp. 20-21; TinnaPong, p. 22 (support); Tatyana Vyc, p. 22 (girls).